B
THAi LEAD

About a Week in Peru That Had
Nothing to Do with Macchu Picchu

HARINI S U

INDIA · SINGAPORE · MALAYSIA

Notion Press

No. 8, 3ʳᵈ Cross Street,
CIT Colony, Mylapore,
Chennai, Tamil Nadu – 600 004

First Published by Notion Press 2021
Copyright © Harini S U 2021
All Rights Reserved.

ISBN 978-1-63806-621-7

For Rakesh,
whose presence and absence both helped me find
the power and strength in words.

CONTENTS

PROLOGUE

March 5, Thursday, 2020

She was the last one to board the flight and by the time she settled in her seat, the flight was ready for takeoff. Even amidst the whirring noise, she could hear her heartbeat. She rested her head and glanced at the roof for a quick second and immediately closed her eyes. Memories of that journey from two years ago flashed on her mind.

Her mind brought back the strange feeling of reading through her chat history with her brother, downloading his pictures from everywhere realizing she would have to live with just his pictures for the rest of her life. She was only twenty-seven and the life in front of her felt very long. It felt odd that the youngest person in the entire family was no more. The thirty-six hours of flight journey back home for her brother's funeral was spent on trying to make sense of life and death. Her only breaks from her phone were for staring at the roof. She would cry for hours looking at the picture and then look at the roof and cry again. Little did she know that she might never be able to look at the roof of a plane normally ever again.

After that dreadful journey, this was her first time traveling alone. Once again, the roof of that plane brought back the face that she missed the most in her life. She opened her eyes and took a deep breath. Inhale… Exhale… Inhale… Exhale…The flight attendant had just finished briefing the safety protocols.

She was traveling to an unknown country to meet unknown people, miles away from familiarity to a remote city in the middle of nowhere. She cursed herself a little for choosing to go on this trip. There are things we do, with absolute clarity and there are things we do with absolute certainty. She was certain she needed this trip. As for clarity, one could not be sure.

Grief comes unannounced but stays the loudest in your head. Also, grief takes an expression so unique that sometimes it does not even make sense. She felt lonely inside for losing her only companion since childhood, yet she was longing to go on a trip all alone. Did her grief push her to go on this trip?

She had a lot of questions about life, her life, what she liked, what she wanted, who she was meant to be, and what she was supposed to do with her time on earth, given it is very short. She was also frustrated because there were no quick answers. Was she going on this journey in search of answers? Was she merely wanting to get away from it all? Or was there something else on her mind?

Cold air blew on her face. Lights went off. She drifted to sleep. Or, so it seemed.

COFFEE TO COCKTAIL

Day 3 – March 8, Sunday, 2020

> *You cannot shake hands with
> a clenched fist.*
>
> Indira Gandhi, First female Prime Minister of India

CHAPTER 1

It was 1 AM. I was on a single bed by the corner of a giant room that had ten other single beds. All lights were off except for three cell phone screens. Everyone was asleep and there was no sound except the air conditioner running. It might have seemed like we were in our own worlds into our screens. But, after a closer look, one would see that we three were chatting with each other, trying so hard to control our laughter over a childhood pic of Karin with a toy dog that she sent for no real reason other than to put a smile on our faces. It had been a while since I laughed like that. Mary Lind (ML) and Karin made me laugh so much that I went to sleep that night in happy tears and grateful stomachache. Even for me, it was hard to believe that we were complete strangers until three days ago when we first met in the dining area of a small hotel in Lima, the capital city of Peru.

Three Days Ago... March 6, Friday, 2020

"I am not much of a coffee drinker, but I am going to try today", said ML. I nodded. I was tired from the long flight and needed an external influence, too.

Anita said something in Spanish, which I did not understand, probably nor did ML. We both took a sip, but I couldn't move past that. Anita tried to explain something again, and this time, ML understood. It was strong espresso-type coffee that had to be mixed with hot water to get to Americano. I am neither American nor a coffee drinker, so I was not surprised about my ignorance. With the coffee-in-Peru 101, my adventure started on a high note.

I call it an adventure because, when I boarded my flight the previous day to Lima, nine other women boarded their flights from different parts of the US to the same destination. All I knew about the trip was that ten strangers including myself would stay together for a week in a remote town in Peru, where English is hardly spoken, to support a group of local women we have never met before. Also, Fair Trade is a relatively new concept to me even now, but I did not know much before the trip. Most of them, my fellow women travelers, were experts in it, as I understood through their introductions over breakfast. If that's not enough, I was the only Indian Chica (girl) in the group. What was I thinking?

CHAPTER 2

My decision to go on this trip was instinctive. I had been wanting to travel alone somewhere, to push myself beyond my comfort zone.

I could have got on a plane to anywhere in the world. But I was not thrilled about getting lost amidst a bunch of tourists. I was too scared to go to a forest or a mountain and be with animals, given I was not confident of my survival skills in the city with humans. I needed the trip to be about something that I deeply cared about, something meaningful. It had to be challenging enough to push me out of my comfort zone yet safe enough, so my parents still have a kid left.

When I was exploring different volunteering options near me, sometime in the summer of 2019, my husband introduced Fair Anita to me. He knew that I was looking for a network to support the cause of 'violence against women'. Founder of Fair Anita, Joy McBrien, and her story inspired him, and I got hooked on everything about Fair Anita right away. So, when Fair Anita announced an opportunity to travel with the founder herself to Peru, the place where it all started, I applied immediately.

About Fair Anita

Fair Anita is a social enterprise with the mission to invest in women around the world. Fair Anita has partnered with about eight thousand talented female artisans in nine countries who make jewelry products and generally earn three times the minimum wage. In 2009, the founder Joy McBrien set out to learn about violence against women in Peru. Peru has one of the world's highest reported domestic violence rates. During the months she spent building a women's shelter in Chimbote, Peru, Joy met many domestic violence survivors and learned about their stories of survival and resilience. These women expressed that jobs are the single most crucial resource for women experiencing domestic violence, knowing that sustainable income would help empower them to leave an abusive partner. Joy founded Fair Anita from the lessons she learned in Chimbote, and to this day, the work remains grounded in supporting women's resilience through responsive business relationships.

Each product comes from 1 of 9 countries, where often women have limited job opportunities. Leaders in these countries organize most groups that work with Fair Anita. Through building artisan groups, artisan partners have access to sustainable income, health insurance, and educational scholarships. Economic independence is key to women's empowerment, given many artisan partners have histories of domestic abuse. When women earn a steady income, they are less dependent on their partner and can more easily support themselves and their children, or they are more respected in their homes, so abuse levels go down.

As you can see, Fair Anita combined businesses, the world I am familiar with, with fair and good, the world I want for all of us. When the opportunity came, to closely understand their business, I had to go for it. After a week of nervously waiting, Joy confirmed that I was on the trip. After several months of waiting, there I was in Peru, living the dream, to begin the most awaited journey. I knew that for the introvert (mostly) in me, especially under grief, spending a week alone with strangers would mean a lot of awkwardness. But there I was anyway, with my awkward coffee-making skills, getting to know others over breakfast.

CHAPTER 3

Around 8 AM, we were all set to check out and catch the bus to Chimbote, the town where we were to spend the week. We reached the bus station after taking several precautions as advised by Joy, such as not taking phones out in a taxi, holding on to our bags with extra caution while walking, etc. Once we checked-in and got our tickets, we met Jessica, the final member of our group at the boarding area. She missed her connecting flight and fortunately made it on time for the bus. We boarded the bus and finally relaxed as the bus started moving. Joy, Anita and the ten of us settled in an extra sophisticated section of the bus that felt almost like a private bus just for ourselves. Tanya and I sat next to each other in the last row. I had met Jessica and Tanya once in a women's networking event in Twin Cities, where I live. When I say 'met', it was a brief 'Hi' followed by some formal exchanges about work, professional interests, events of that evening, etc. But here, Tanya and I were sitting next to each other, about to spend the next 6+ hours together.

Once the bus picked up speed, and the group started winding down slowly, some of them took naps, ML started working on her laptop, Joy, and Anita were discussing plans for the week and others' actions I do not remember registering. Tanya and I took our books out to read. Not sure how the conversation started, but within minutes, we talked about some interesting topics such as relationships, women in corporate, our views about women's choice to have kids, etc. I connected quickly with her due to our similarities in a lot of ways. Just like any human who finds peace in familiarity, I found myself getting some peace, too. Somewhere deep down, this provided some assurance that after all, I might not just survive this experience, but possibly even create some friendships.

After alternating desert and coastline topographies, some more conversations, a not-sure-what-it's-called vegetarian lunch, and short-lived naps, we reached Chimbote.

About Chimbote

Before my first-ever travel to Peru, I did not know much about the country. Before I came across Fair Anita, I did not know anything about Chimbote as well. So, I owe you the imaginary gears you need to visualize our journey in and around Chimbote across the next few days in the following chapters.

Most of us know that Lima, from where we took the bus to Chimbote, is Peru's capital. It is also the largest city in Peru, housing one-third of Peru's population. Chimbote is situated roughly six hours away from Lima and about two hundred and fifty miles north of Lima. For a sense of familiarity, Chimbote is approximately a thousand miles away from Macchu Picchu.

Peru consists of three different terrains – flat coastal areas that are mostly desert, steep mountains in the center, and rainforest in the east that receive rainfall between November to April. Chimbote, located in Peru's coastal areas, is very dry with little to no rainfall for the majority of the year. All along our bus journey from Lima to Chimbote, we observed the changing terrains throughout. I later got to understand that this diversity in terrains could bring both favorable and unfavorable conditions for the population in this region.

Chimbote is home to more than 400,000 people, many of whom live in extreme poverty. It looked like any other developing country with small shops along the streets, many pedestrians walking by the roadside, some parts of the town clean and some not, sounds of life bustling, and the smell of dry summer in parts taken over occasionally by the smell of coastal fishes. I even felt a bit nostalgic because of these similarities with parts of India. Chimbote being a relatively bigger town in comparison, the everyday clothing and food were not very different from what we see modern men and women wear across the world.

It is hard to get a taxi and especially get safe transports. So, Joy pre-arranged a van with a known driver who could safely commute us to our place of stay. With everyone on board, the van drove us along the streets of Chimbote.

CHAPTER 4

Taking in the vibes of Chimbote, we reached our destination. Even before the van entered the Parish parking, we could hear loud music. The energy and enthusiasm were so high and contagious. The vibrance and warmth I have experienced in several south American cultures were immediately felt by every one of us. They received us all with colorful balloons, multiple dance moves, engaging music, and the banners that proudly said FAIR ANITA.

After a terrific duo performance from Joy and Anita, the party momentarily came to an end, so that we could get checked-in before heading to a more personal introduction with the artisan women in their workshop space. The place we stayed in was a large room lined with ten beds in dorm-style next to each other. We randomly chose our beds and settled our luggage. We knew going into the trip that the ten of us will share one big room. But I did not pay attention to the fact that we were also going to share one bathroom. Sounds like fun? Yes, it was. Anyway, we did not have time to digest any of this, as we immediately headed out to the workshop. Walking along the streets of Chimbote, especially the parts where we lived, gave a closer look at the houses there. I also learned that the well-constructed and painted homes in that neighborhood did not necessarily provide an accurate representation of the economic conditions of people living inside. The government built houses as a part of their developmental projects, but the employment situation did not improve. So, even though people have a place to live, they might not necessarily have the means to lead a sustainable life in the house.

After walking a couple of blocks, we reached the workshop. The workshop was a small shed, an extension of one of Peru's artisan women's houses. Maritza's daughter welcomed us with a yummy welcome cocktail as we settled into chairs. The cocktail name was Macchu Picchu that contained Pisco (Peruvian alcoholic drink), orange juice, and Grenadine syrup made with such precision that the three layers stayed separate. I did not know that I was supposed to stir the drink to mix all three layers before drinking. What was the purpose of spending all that effort creating three layers if all I had to do was mix it all anyway? So, I drank as such. So did ML, who was sitting next to me. As we were sipping our cocktails, Joy had planned an ice breaker activity to help us and the artisans remember all our names. We were to enact a pose or show a symbol while saying our names, so others can visually remember our names. My name in Hindi means deer. So, I made a deer-like pose in the best way I can. I think it worked because even at the end of the trip, most of them remembered the symbol and my name. After the activity, the artisan women at the workshop shared some highlights of their life stories. Some of them were brief, some of them elaborate, some with a smile, and some with tears; it was too much to take in, in a too-short period of time. It was too much, not because of the amount of information but because of how different each of their lives was. Their path to get there included fighting against several odds such as disability, lack of resources, violence, lack of support from the government, a lot of hope, and a few strong leaders, both men, and women. I felt pity first. Then I felt uncomfortable because my life was better than theirs for no specific reason.

Halfway through the stories, ML and I realized that the drink's bottom-most layer was Grenadine, which tasted bitter, and that's why we were supposed to mix the layers before drinking. Guess we both are not the best drinkers of anything. We both looked at each other and instantly let out a big laugh realizing what we did. Our not-so-silent laughter also lightened up the room.

CHAPTER 5

We headed back to our room for dinner. This was our first meal in Chimbote. We had a designated room with a dining table and chairs. Two women from the local community cooked fresh food for us and served it at our dining table. Food was also tailor-made for vegetarians that included steamed vegetables, rice, and potato along with meat options for others.

Dinner was followed by a reflection activity conducted by Tanya and Joy. Tanya and Joy are college buddies, both so inspiring that they used to volunteer together and organize events like this jointly.

Their team effort and intentional reflection activities were nothing but short of pure positivity. One final task for the night was for each of us to pick a buddy from the group. Buddies were to spend reflection time at the end of each day to share the highs and lows of the day and to help process emotions during the trip in a healthy way. The primary intent of this system was to create a safe and trusted space for conversations that we otherwise could not share in front of ten other people. Tanya and I became buddies for each other instantly from our bonding earlier in the day. We headed upstairs to the open verandah next to our room, which our group renamed as poor man's patio in the days to come.

Tanya and I are both deep into our corporate jobs, with a common intent to create an impact for people around us yet coming from two different cultures far apart from each other. I was also inspired by her bias for action and how much difference she was creating with her volunteering activities across several local businesses and leadership in networks that work for women empowerment, climate change, and other leading concerns. We discussed women in corporate, family, bias, societal expectations, and many more as we were joined by Jessica. Jessica is another inspiring leader, a skilled communicator, and a lot more, with a focused intent to drive social impact. Also, she is an avid traveler who brings a lot of fun to the conversations. Shortly, Joy and few others joined us for an extended first long night in Chimbote, which couldn't have started better.

The moon shone brightly in the sky as everyone went to bed. I went to my bed but couldn't fall asleep. Sharing a bathroom meant that I either had to wake up too soon or too late to get some extra time there to get ready. I decided to be the last one to wake up, given that itself meant waking up at 8 AM. This gave me an excuse to stay up for another hour or so, and I started journaling. For a structured person like me, it was a strange experience to see myself writing down a bunch of puzzling questions and unfinished sentences. But I kept writing until it was too late. I would have gone to bed sooner and recharged myself better if I knew what was about to come the next day.

TEARS TO TENACITY

Day 2 – March 7, Saturday, 2020

> *Freedom cannot be achieved unless women have been emancipated from all forms of oppression.*
>
> Nelson Mandela

CHAPTER 6

Our first morning in Chimbote, started at 5 AM for me with a rumbling stomach. I was woken up by sickness, and I thank all gods even today for making me sick at the right time when all the stars were perfectly aligned. Why? Because the restroom was available. I later came to know that our friend Jessica missed the opportunity by a few minutes and had to struggle to get the restroom downstairs open. I did not know any of this at that time when I was inside. And her version of how her first morning in Chimbote started, I am certain, would look vastly different.

With lack of sleep and physical discomfort, I set out with my fellow women to spend the first half of the day touring some of Chimbote's neighborhoods. We were led by Anita, the boss lady, who seemed to know every single person in the community. We also had a couple of translators, Claudia and Adrian, so we do not miss out on forming connections because of language barriers.

We walked to our first stop, which was introduced to us as Quintas. These are community houses with multiple small houses built inside a single complex shared by several families. These were built by Father Jack for the new parents who were living with their parents and probably other siblings in a small house. Quintas were intended to provide space and a safe community for the growth of the next generation. We stopped next to a building that was once an active home for older adults who needed medical care. Anita explained how the state of this facility had changed with the changing political conditions. The building was currently in a sad state that lacked any facilities for elderly care. As we walked through the streets, several times Father Jack's name came up, showcasing the significant impacts he has had on the development of this community. We also stopped by a house where they were making furniture from Bamboos, which was their primary source of income, no different from what I had seen in Indian small towns and villages.

It was hard not to draw parallels to the similarities between India and Peru, maybe even a few other developing countries I have visited. The social structures, physical structures, approach toward family, and relationships are some examples. This familiar feeling made me less prepared for what I was about to experience for the rest of that day.

CHAPTER 7

During this tour, I started talking to one of the fellow women from our group, Karin. Karin and her husband are world travelers and professional photographers. They also found a way to combine their passion for photography to create an impact on the world. In her introduction, she had shared about one of her projects 'Big Picture', which touched me deeply. The couple traveled to remote parts of the world to teach individuals of varied ages and circumstances, the basic use of camera and concepts of photography. They started this project so the local community, stripped away from the rest of the world could learn to capture their own lives the way they wanted to be remembered. "Because who better knows their life than themselves?" She had said. During that project period, she also realized that these families from communities that have gone through several traumatic events such as war, political changes, natural disasters, etc. did not have a record of their past lives. So, as an extension of the project, they collaborated with partner organizations to generate donations as well as print the photos they have captured as a gift to the families so they can honor their memories for generations to come.

I was intrigued to ask her more about it because of my internal search to bring the worlds of art and social change together within my own life, I started asking about her experience, her story, her ideas on how I can make sense of my quest for art and talked about how I can give back to the world. In a way, I can say that my decision to write this book was inspired by her stories and ideas. Karin and I connected easily through humor and art in the following days, but as I look back at that particular day, that was one inspiring memory of the day that I cherish till date.

As we kept walking, one thing I noticed was how the landscape kept changing, rather gradually worsening as we went deeper into the town. I was already made aware at the beginning of the day, that we were to visit some of the poorest parts of the town. But it was one thing to 'know' but completely another thing to 'see'.

CHAPTER 8

Anita is famous and recognized by almost everyone in the neighborhood. Fair Anita is named after her, she was a social worker in Chimbote when Joy met her for the first time. Anita is a fearless leader, who knows how to drive real-time change on the ground. Senora Anita, as locals call her, is a strong believer that women who lead, are the real changemakers in the world. We felt like royals walking alongside her in the community that celebrated her as queen.

As a part of her daily routine, she casually takes a walk around the street and stops by at a house to check upon them. This helps her stay updated on who needed support, what kind of help they needed and when it was needed. Based on her survey, she would prioritize the resources that she receives for community development.

This was one such visit, where she casually stopped at a house and was talking with a woman. After few minutes, we were asked to come in so that we could see the house. As soon as we entered, I was shocked by the stark contrast between the outside of the house and the inside. Amidst the damaged floor, feeble asbestos roof, and dirt-loaded walls, was an older man sitting on a chair. He spoke in Spanish to Anita in a shaky voice that was translated to us by Joy. We got to know that he was abandoned by his family after he was paralyzed physically. He did not have anyone with him now. He lived under the care of his neighbors who check-in on him and provided him with his basic needs as much as they could afford to share. He also said that he was really scared of living there in case it rained, as his place would give up within few hours.

Peru is a disaster-prone region with several environmental phenomena working adversely against the population there. The coastal regions of Peru especially are subjected to natural disasters such as El Nino, Earthquakes, and many more. Chimbote is dry throughout the year but when they get rainfall as a side-effect of El Nino, it always results in the flood with severe damages to the community. In March 2017, they experienced ten times more rainfall than normal resulting in historic floods and affected more than seventy thousand households as reported by the Business Insider.

His eyes and the pain they reflected can never be erased from my mind. I wish no one in their old age live in fear, not just about death, but about the helplessness to protect themselves from day-to-day life.

As Anita consoled him that she would reach out to him soon, we all slowly got off his house. My mind was occupied with multiple thoughts that I was not able to structure. I grew up in India for twenty-five years of my life. India is a developing country and poverty is not a new sight to me either. I have seen people living on huts, people in slums, and poor people who begged for money on the streets. Ideally, I should not have been affected by this sight in Peru. But I was and I did not know why. Have I changed so much in the few years that I stayed away from India? I do not know the answer yet. But I think we do not always absorb information the same way. I understand now that depending on where I was at that point in life, my conscious mind related to different things and remembered different things.

In the days to come, Julia and I dwelled upon how we processed these experiences differently. Julia has also traveled to Cambodia with Fair Anita on a similar trip. And yet, her decision to go to Peru to allow herself to be torn by such experiences once again gave me a different perspective to process my own emotions.

While we were there in those hot, sandy, streets of Chimbote, I was also reminded of what it meant to live in a disaster zone like that. I grew up in different parts of India with widely different topographies. When I was 4-5 years old, our family lived in Andaman island, which was and is prone to earthquakes. The need to be on a constant alert when you sense a symptom of tremor is widely underestimated if one has not experienced it. But Chennai, the place I called home for most of my life, was not supposed to be a disaster zone. Yet the 2015 Chennai floods shook the city in a way never before. Families were stuck in their homes without food, electricity, transportation, lost all their belongings, and in some cases their lives as well. Since that disaster, every December, even a moderate rainfall causes the kind of terror that reminds them of the worst that went by. This is no different from Florida hurricanes or California wildfires. The common denominator is that all disasters affect the poor the most. And being in this poorest of the neighborhoods, it hit me hard to know the reality they live in each day.

CHAPTER 9

Before I could finish my trail of thoughts on that topic, we stopped at another house. As usual, Anita went inside first and was talking to an older man there. But this time, two little girls, aging around 8-10 years came out of the house. They did not know English. Their eyes full of curiosity and excitement to see new faces from a faraway world. They were shy to talk, yet I could tell, they wanted to talk. I was wondering what would be going on in their little heads, looking at us strangers outside their doorstep. One of the girls went close to Joy and started talking. She asked something in Spanish and Joy replied. I thought she recognized Joy from her previous visits to Chimbote. But the girl did something that I did not expect. She started going around the circle, asking a question to each woman in our group. I asked Joy what the girl was asking, as I wanted to make sure I reply when it comes to me. The answer I heard from Joy shocked me. I kept asking myself if my mind was dramatically exaggerating that situation. I am not sure. So, I am going to leave it up to you, the readers, to decide.

I got to know that she was asking Joy, "Do you have a boyfriend? Are you married? Do you have kids?" She was going around the circle asking, "How many kids do you have?" When it came to my turn, I just shook my head indicating "None". But the silence in me prolonged for a long time after we left the house. As we left the house to walk toward the Parish, Anita was explaining that there were four girls in the house. Their mother died and their father abandoned them. They lived with their grandfather, the older man in the house, but the community was afraid that those girls might have to end up sharing the bed with him if they do not get a secure separated space in the house. So, Anita wanted to check on their condition, so she could plan on supporting them when she can divert resources there.

As a child, I had a lot of dreams. Whenever a guest was home and asked me what I wanted to become when I grew up, I would tell them different answers each time. I wanted to be a musician for a long time, then a doctor, then a civil servant, then a dancer, the list makes one really curious to know who I eventually became. Well, I ended up a sandwiched version of my dreams and what society made me believe as reality. But what matters, is that I knew how to dream, which meant even as an adult, however, conditioned I become, there is still a possibility that I could dream. That I would have the privilege to know how it felt to dream beyond limitations.

On the other hand, the same guests who fueled my dreams until I was a kid, started talking about marriage as

I started growing up to be a woman. I clearly remember the disappointment I felt.

And I felt that again in this situation. What was I disappointed at? I have no idea. At the small girl? Or, at the design of this world that reduced the curiosity of that small girl's mind to kids and marriage? I was sad for her. I kept wondering if she dreamed of other things for her. I was also angry deep down but could not pinpoint the reason. I just walked the rest of the way in silence, back to my temporary nest, my bed.

Thank god, the day did not end there.

CHAPTER 10

We had a jewelry workshop that afternoon, where we learned to make a bracelet from the scratch. My grandmother used to teach me crochet work when I was a kid. She was so busy her entire life attending to my grandfather and his needs and raising five kids, yet she never gave up on her crochet. Whenever I used to ask her why she was exhausting herself making crochets when she could be resting in the short break she gets, she used to tell me that everyone, especially women, needs some form of art or craft in their everyday routine. When I asked why she told me that it is a world that belonged only to her imaginations, she replied that it takes away her mind from every problem she has at that moment and helps her refuel herself. I might not be as crafty as her, but she might be the reason why arts and crafts get me excited always. This bracelet-making workshop did the same magic for me, the crochet did for my grandma. It took me away from my muddled mind for a brief period.

The bonding and warmth of the artisan women cheered me up further. Maria and Rosario helped me string the beads, Ruby helped me tie it all together and Elena created a hand-carved tag for the bracelet that read 'POWER'.

I was thankful for this distraction that I got a break from the experiences of that morning. I also realized why that was a happy place for those women. That was their world. They ruled the beads. That was where they got lost in something beyond their everyday lives. That was art. The sympathy and pity I felt on Day 1 for artisan women and their stories shifted to a strong sense of admiration that day, as I closely looked at their work and their expertise in what they do.

The sights I saw that morning made me feel happy for the artisan women, who were getting paid three times more than minimum wage through Fair Anita and were leading an example for several women in the community with a constant dream of improving their standard of life. I was even more proud of the work Fair Anita was doing there to get those women the global platform they needed.

We ended the night with dinner and the much-needed reflection activity and buddy chat. All of that, helped in reducing the intensity of my confusion and frustration, yet, nothing made the one question in my mind go away – Who was to blame?

Wandering in those thoughts, counting my privileges, somewhere in the darkness, I drifted to sleep.

INDIFFERENCE TO CONVICTION

Day 3 — March 8, Sunday, 2020

> *I alone cannot change the world.*
> *But I can cast a stone across the waters to*
> *create many ripples.*

Mother Teresa

CHAPTER 11

Day 3, March 8th, International Women's Day was the focus of the day. I never celebrated this day because I never knew the difference this day could make.

I was fifteen years old when I was first groped in a public street in a broad daylight by an unknown face. I remembered feeling ashamed as if it was my mistake. I remembered walking in fear the whole way that day. I remembered all the days and the nights I have had to walk in fear. I remembered having my brother, my dad, or my friends who are all the decent men in my life, shielding me against those evil men lurking in public places to grab at anything they could get. I remembered thinking of all those women, who did not have a man in their life to shield, a car to travel, an option to stay home and be protected like an expensive property that I felt like sometimes. I also remembered Nirbhaya and many others before and after her. I remembered my mother and my mother's mother, directly and indirectly, protecting me from men around, silently letting me know that they remembered, too. When I have no way of forgetting any of the above, when all kinds of violence are being committed against women every single minute of the day throughout the year, across the world, what is the point of this one day anyway? But this year, I was forced to celebrate that in Peru for the artisan women and their families. I decided to go along with the plan.

CHAPTER 12

We went on a local picnic with the women and their families to a theme park nearby. I learned that for many of them, this was a rare occasion where they go out as a family.

Out of the artisan partners Fair Anita works with, some of them are physically challenged and others have kids or family members that are physically challenged. With the everyday struggle, they have to perform day-to-day activities, which we take for granted, having a picnic as a family was a rare occasion.

As we reached the park, it took us an hour to get everyone out of the two buses that were hired for the day. We gradually moved along the park until we found a space for us with some shadow so we could spend some quality time chatting and have lunch. The women had cooked lunch for all of us. As everyone started settling down, some of them started arranging plates and cups for lunch. ML, yes, my drink buddy, and I got more time to connect this day. She was conversing in Spanish to the extent she knew, with one of the artisan women. Given my Spanish skills are below basic, I joined her in the conversation in the spirit of getting to know the women further and in full confidence that ML will be able to translate it for me. Gradually the conversation went toward family, kids, grandkids, then us showing pictures of our families to them. After some time, we started serving lunch to the families and we also settled down to eat.

Maybe this is a good time to tell you about my food experience on this trip as well. I already talked about the amount of preparation that went into arranging our stay. A key part of that was food. They not only made sure to accommodate three vegetarians in the group, but also ensured to provide nutritious meal filled with a healthy dose of vegetables, protein, and carbs for all three meals. The reason I wanted to talk about food there is that the lunch made by the women was one of many factors that made me feel close to their culture. It was rice with vegetables, corn, and potato with some spices, which tasted very close to the Pulao in India. This combined with Inca-cola made for a happy lunch. Marissa, ML, Tanya, Adrian, and I sat at a table, dug deep into our lunch plates, and recharged ourselves.

As we were wrapping up our lunch, a cute little girl from one of the families wanted to play on the trampoline and needed one of us to accompany her. Some of us got up to give her company and I thought we were going to stand there and watch her play. ML left with the kid first, while I collected my handbag and followed them. As I went near the trampoline, I realized that ML had other plans. She became a kid herself and started jumping on the trampoline with the kid. Their energies were so contagious, that I had to go on that too. Thankfully, it was a huge trampoline that could hold us all in a place. Soon, few other kids joined us and kicked both of us out to have the trampoline space for themselves. Laughter can instantly connect people together and I saw that happen in my case with ML. ML is a woman leader with a range of life and career experiences. She is currently in sales and customer service for a different Fair-Trade organization. Her personal life is filled with multi-cultural family and travel experiences, which she brings to the conversation in her own humorous style. She was the eldest in our group I think but according to me, the most energetic member of our group. If I could be half as enthusiastic about life as she is when I grow physically older, I will consider my life to be a success.

As some of the kids in the group wanted to visit the zoo, we ventured out to see some birds and animals, eventually landing in a swimming pool. As I write this in a time when COVID-19 is at its peak in the US, the image of a swimming pool with so many humans next to each other in a small space feels so alienated. I am going to hold the visual of this memory so strong in the hopes that the universe can get us all back to being in swimming pools again someday.

On that day though, I was not planning on getting inside the pool. Julia, Sarah, and I stayed outside the pool, watching the rest of the group having fun and helping document those memories through our cameras. Karin, the official photographer of our group, unfortunately, had to miss this event as she was sick. While we were taking pictures of the pool fun, Julia took her art travel journal out so that she could record that memory in an extra special way. The first word that comes to my mind when I think of Julia is 'Sweet'. She is quiet and cheerful and an artist with a lot of love for Fair Trade. I can confidently say that one of my most pleasant experiences during the week was to watch Julia do her magic in her art journal.

For some of them, this was their first time getting into a pool. Their face and ear-to-ear smile said it all loud and clear. The incredible women from our group made it possible for physically abled and women with special needs alike to enjoy the pool experience and I thought and hoped that that would be a memorable day in their lives.

After some time, I joined Maria and Anita, who were dancing to the live music by the pool. We danced for hours because, when Anita dances, you just cannot simply stand and watch. So, after hours of dancing, soaking myself in sweat, and getting a little more burned by the sun, I finally decided to go back and sit. This day with them, getting to know their families, seeing them as their casual selves, not only increased my admiration but also brought a sense of connection with them. We realized that it was already 4 PM, so we packed our bags, boarded our buses back to drop the families off.

Our day though did not end yet.

CHAPTER 13

A special plan was baked into this evening for us after the drop-offs. And that was to head to a beach nearby. Honestly, I was not expecting anything as the scenery along the way to the beach was mostly that of a mid-sized town with shops everywhere till we were about ten minutes away from the beach. Our bus took a sharp left and suddenly, the topography looked completely different. We got down and walked for a few minutes and voila! We had our own private beach now. And even more perfect? Sun was starting to go down in between the mountains. I was expecting the ocean and sun, but the mountains were a bonus. Some of us sat there, some were taking pictures, some headed out to the beach. Something about me always attracted people who love horror stories, though I have never watched a single horror movie with both my eyes open. Claudia, one of the two translators, joined us for this fun evening, and shared her real-life horror stories she experienced around that beach. Overall, it was a beautiful evening of conversations, picture-perfect lights, and scenery to capture our faces filled with smiles.

That was I think the first pause for me in the past three days. A much-needed slowdown. I think subconsciously I was stressed. My periods were delayed, my appetite levels changed, starting stages of sunburn and an uncooperative tummy were some of the symptoms to show that my body was stressed at the least. So, this pause meant a lot to me, to my body, to my mind. That was probably the first moment in those three days that I could recognize any of this consciously in front of the vastness ahead. On a stressful day, when you run and burn all your energy, the resulting state of mind is somewhat close to the state of a puppy after playtime. A sense of calm, peace, and clarity in a strangely tiring way. When all the energy you have is sucked out of your body, your mind is no longer fueled to churn. And then, all of a sudden, you see things for what they are.

I felt distant yet close with all these women I made friends in just three days, as I sat there watching the sun go down. While I was sitting there watching others, I noticed something else, too. As the sun started going further down, the women in different colors and appearances started fading and slowly all I could see was their silhouettes. These black outlines could be different in size, shape, height, but they all were captured as silhouettes when the light was against the lens. We all could be coming from different worlds, fighting different battles, living different lives yet all of us were connected by a common thread. We were all there together because all of us felt the need to fight against something that was not right about this world. And that something, I realized, was patriarchy.

The definition of patriarchy is that it is a social system that is developed in a way that men hold power and domination in terms of political leadership, authority, power over morals, social privileges, and control of the land. There are men in all of our lives who we despise. They lack respect for women, refuse to believe in gender equality, take advantage of and exploit women. We also see good, respectable, decent men who are active advocates of gender equality. I also have such men. My father who shares household work, my husband who moved to another country in support of my career, my friends who take care, do everything they can to support their sister, wife, mother in pursuing their dreams. So, though I am pro-woman, I am not anti-men.

But, as I started getting out of my social definitions of who I was supposed to be, and started becoming the woman and the person I wanted to be, I started noticing that the men in my life were struggling to cope with my changes. The more vocal I became in terms of my views toward women's rights, the harder it was for them to understand what I was talking about when it comes to the gender gap. That's when I realized that this is not about good and bad men. This is about a societal structure that has defined what is good and bad for each gender and made us all believe it. If you coincidentally or out of your own will fit into those definitions of good and bad, you might have never had to doubt the structure. And that structure is called patriarchy.

Black Lives Matter leaders say that "It is not enough to not be a racist, you have to be actively anti-racist".

Because, the dial in the balance is on the extreme side toward white supremacy structures, favoring the white, and the collective society has to become actively anti-racist to shift the balance and bring it back to the neutral position. Similarly, I learned that it is not enough to advocate for gender equality. As a society, that was built on patriarchal principles, if we were to truly achieve gender equality, we need to become actively 'anti-patriarchy'.

If patriarchy was built by men for men, then why should men fight against it? Because the seeping impacts of patriarchy on our modern lives today are no longer just on women. It exists in all forms of toxic masculinity against men. The good men I call in my life were and are going through a lot of criticisms based on false notions around their gender roles and expectations. My brother used to be someone who hardly cried in front of others. My friend was constantly criticized as a kid for being kind and gentle. Another friend was judged for earning less than his wife. Even women are guilty of making judgmental comments about some men who we think do not fit into the social definitions of how men are supposed to be.

Men could have found patriarchy and its rules to create power dynamics against women. The gender roles were probably set in a way to make sure women were focused on nurturing and growing the human race forward. Yet, even after burdening the earth with more than required humans, women are not relieved from their responsibilities to their race. Patriarchy wanted women to believe that we are nothing more than our uterus and vaginas and unfortunately, this irrelevant sexist ideology exists even today in a sneaky invisible way. And that is how patriarchy has been having the power to hold men and women in invisible cuffs for thousands of years.

Think of patriarchy as a wall built by a small group of men several years ago, which was conveniently guarded by generations of men. The men and women for generations strongly believed and still believe that the wall protected them. Smart men realized that the rigid wall was not only crushing women but also their own hands. Other men still continued to believe in the wall and got their hands, and sometimes even their heads crushed.

The trickiest yet the most impactful ideology that patriarchy ended up creating is to define masculinity and femineity. And we as the human race have been trying so hard to live up to those definitions, but most of us die trying. The reality however is, today and always, we had, and we have people with varying shades of masculine and feminine characters. As the population grew, humans living in all different shades of the gender spectrum grew. There is no sense talking black and white when it comes to gender. Real talk happens when we see the gray area. And the gray area cannot be seen unless the rigid walls of patriarchy are broken.

As the artisan women we met, fight bead-by-bead for their families, Anita fights for the economic independence of several such women. While Joy fights for violence against women, Tanya, Jessica, and many others like me fight for equality in corporate. As each of us fights for our space, to be seen, to be heard, to be let to live our own lives, to be treated as equals, I believed that slowly but gradually, we were breaking that wall down, one tiny brick at a time. Can we break the wall altogether with blunt force? Maybe yes if more people stop guarding the wall and switch sides. But until then, why stop breaking the tiny bricks if we can?

If we need 'Earth Day' to remind ourselves that earth needs to be celebrated and 'Valentine's Day' to remind ourselves that love needs to be celebrated, I was convinced that, 'Women's Day' was much needed.

SUNBURN TO SUNSET

Day 4 – March 9, Monday, 2020

> *Only a life lived for*
> *others is worth living.*
>
> Albert Einstein

CHAPTER 14

What is the common thread that connects construction, crayons, and cocktails? Think… Think…Think…Nothing? Partially right! This day is the only thread that can connect these three unrelated events in our experiences.

We started the day volunteering to help build a house for a local single mother with two kids. Part of the money we paid for the trip went into sponsoring this house for them. This is the value of partnering with organizations like Fair Anita that provides visibility and confidence to the money we spend on them. I was excited to see that coming to reality in front of our eyes. Most of us sat in a cubicle and worked in front of a computer all day. We were all excited to get some physical work done. We had a fun ride at the back of an open truck to the construction site. The original plan was that the roof will be done by the time we arrived, and we were to paint the walls and help organize the things back into the house. But the contractors at the site were running late to get the roof fixed. This meant that we had to wait outside for a couple of hours until it was done. I carried the sunburns from the previous day. I have brown skin, I lived in the southern part of India all my life, which has tropical weather year around. If I burned my skin, it means that the sun was beyond brutal and this construction site and the perimeter around had no shade. Anita wanted to take us on a mini tour around the neighborhood by the time we waited, so we need not stand in the sun. She walked us through the streets around the house we were building, which were predominantly dry with minimal trees. The whole terrain was parched, hot and as you might have rightly guessed, access to water was a problem that most households in this community faced. Anita shared a lot of stories about the political climate in Peru and how corruption, volatility, and lack of access to resources deeply impacted the community. This part of the city looked entirely different from the one visited close to the Parish on Day 2, yet the harsh living conditions were a commonality across. With bits and pieces of shade here and there, we survived on our water bottles for thirst and managed to complete the walking tour to get back to the construction site. The roof was still not done, but we decided to paint the walls of one room that was close to completion. The only problem with that was we would stand in the sun, with no roof, i.e. no shade. I wanted to paint despite my physical conditions because I wouldn't have the opportunity to do it elsewhere. DIY culture is more common in the US, not so much in metropolitan cities in India because of the ample availability of any kind of labor in India to outsource. So, I started painting the walls along with few others. The family that was going to be living in that house was full of hope and excitement and that made our group enthusiastic to create that house for the family. Ideally, we were supposed to paint and help them move their things into the house, but we were happy with the progress though we could not see the final state of the house.

After some time, the priest from the Parish came to check-in on the house and offered to drive some of us back. I took the opportunity to get out of the sun and head to our Parish. Notice, how the Parish became 'our' Parrish now. This was the stage of appreciating and embracing the Parish as my comfort place because I had a bed, some cool air, and a bathroom I can most of the time access.

Marissa, Karin, and I came back to the room as we were all not feeling well one way or the other and got ourselves the much-needed shower and a siesta.

With a rustling sound near me, I woke up and realized that the rest of the group was back. Not only that, we were to get ready for the next activity for the day which was to conduct art classes for local kids. I got up refreshed and feeling energized for rest of the day. These tiny details might seem trivial for some of you and you might wonder why it is even important for me to share that I took a nap. It is important because the agenda of the trip was thoughtfully constructed so we could experience and understand what it means to live in Chimbote. While the harsh weather did impact me physically, the support of both the community that hosted us as well as the group of women I was with constantly lifted each other up.

CHAPTER 15

As I said in previous chapters, I love art but not sure if art loves me back. I can likely say the same thing about kids as well. So, as one can understand, art classes for kids were not in my natural design. Luckily, the wonderful people I was with, all volunteered to be with the kids individually to monitor and help them complete the drawing sheets Julia had put together. She patiently drew some sketches for the kids to color and I helped with logistics such as distributing papers, pens, candies (maybe the only time kids loved me)! Just when I was about to settle down with a sigh of relief, there came this tiny cute fellow who wanted to draw but he did not have any open tables. So, Joy made me sit with him assuming I would help him find art interesting. I am glad no one took a video of what that kid and I drew for an hour. And I am glad this moment was not significant enough for anyone else to notice as they were all engrossed in all the good work going on. That hour felt like my entire life and the poor kid stuck with me would have probably felt the same. Just when I thought I successfully managed to win his attention, there was another kid who also wanted to join me. I offered to take him to someone else, so he didn't have to endure my painful artistic skills. But he insisted on joining me. I drew something, he drew something, he didn't know English, I didn't know Spanish. It would have probably been hilarious if someone else were looking at us. The kid finally understood that he can find better use of his time by teaching me to make a rocket from the paper in which we were scribbling for so long. I welcomed that idea because that felt like a better use of my paper too. Other than my side stint, the kids received the class well and enjoyed it. These are kids from the local community who were going back to school after the break and it was good timing for us to be there and meet them.

CHAPTER 16

Feeling so proud of myself for getting through the art class, I was looking forward to our next and final plan for the day – to experience the tourist side of Chimbote. The first stop was at the boardwalk to experience Chimbote's fishing bay. We were running a little bit late. By now, my group of women knew very well how much I loved sunsets and they were all willing to walk extra fast so we could get there on time for the sunset. ML, jokingly, termed it as our walk with 'purpose' and the purpose was served as we reached the bay on time to see the sunset. The roads leading to the bay opened up to a beautiful ocean view with people with their families walking peacefully by the ocean. The sky was clear but there was mild smog across the surroundings.

Until the 1960s, Chimbote bay was known for clean, blue waters convenient for fishing vessels and densely populated with rich marine life. Very soon, multiple fish and fish processing factories opened up and attracted a population from all over Peru. According to World Bank data, Peru is home to one of the largest anchoveta populations. This species supplies fish oil rich in omega-3 and fishmeal for livestock (meat industry) and aquaculture (Salmon) feeding. Chimbote is the world's top producer of fishmeal with nineteen percent of the world fishmeal being produced there.

Consequently, overfishing, unethical, and unsustainable processes resulted in a devastating amount of reduction in anchoveta population along with severe water and land pollution. This created imbalance in the ocean food chain affecting other species in water, thereby affecting the livelihood and food consumption of humans in the city who were dependent on the easily available seafood for their livelihood. Only in 2009, the Peru government intervened to restrict and govern the fishing industry which to some extent has reduced the depletion of anchoveta and other key species. The sight of this beautiful bay that carried the sad history of few greedy humans did hurt.

We were walking by the ocean trying to find the perfect spot to sit down and have our dinner while we watch the sunset. And suddenly someone casually asked, "Do you know that the whole island in front of you is bird poop?" I sincerely thought that was a prank until I googled and was shocked to know that it was true. The small islands in front of the bay looked like hills but were fact volcanic mountains that appeared white due to the deposition of seabird excreta. Isla Blanca, the largest of the island is an ecological and tourist reserve that preserves guano.

I also learned that Peru is the world's largest producer of guano (excrement of seabirds and bats) which is one of the richest sources of natural fertilizer. Did you know that there were wars fought over the possession of these islands in Peru? I mean, I had to laugh at all the shit (literally) humans have waged wars over. According to Audubon, "When Peruvians first started harvesting guano more than a century ago, the hard-packed dung was up to 200 feet deep. Extraction quickly ate away at the deposits". How do we as a race manage to stay greedy for thousands of years? Once again, with the growing demand for organic and natural fertilizers, the government put strict measures in place that ensured the birds were not disturbed during the extraction process as well as to enforce upper limits on extraction volumes so the resources are not depleted.

For the second day in a row, watching that gorgeous sun go down by the ocean was magical but also sad. That bay should have been a lot more beautiful, a lot less polluted and so should the life of people who are living there.

CHAPTER 17

After the sunset and a lot of pictures, we headed to a local cart for churros. When this bunch of us were selected for this trip, Joy arranged a conference call to discuss the agenda, plan, and preparation. Since that day, I am sure she must have been waiting for this day. If you asked Wikipedia, a churro is a friendly dough pastry that originated in Spain and Portugal. If you asked Joy, churros at that place was love, filled with caramel, that originates and ends in pure bliss (that's my version of describing the excitement she felt to have us taste her favorite churros). If you are imagining some places like Mike's Pastry in Boston for Cannoli or Ghirardelli square in San Francisco for Chocolate, you are mistaken, just like me. It was rather the infamous roadside Pani Puri shop in Mumbai or Delhi, which tourists will not recognize because it is not in Trip advisors and Yelps of the world. But the locals will proudly take you there as though it is a speakeasy bar for which they hold special passwords. We stopped at this small roadside cart, in which the churros were being made fresh and hot. Once you take a bite of the churros, then you know that Joy is officially a local member of Chimbote, because it indeed was the best churros I have ever had. I cannot share the address of this place with you because I do not know, and you cannot find it on Google. If you want to know, you should know from the best, so please ask Joy.

CHAPTER 18

After the churros, we walked by the busy streets of downtown Chimbote filled with shops, roadside carts selling everything under the sun. Another place where I thought for a moment that I was in India. We walked into a fancy bar around 7 PM. I did not see people drinking at 7 PM in Peru, maybe because people were probably working still or their definition of a party was to stay up all night, so they started drinking late in the night. It was also maybe because this place was a bit fancier which means it was expensive for most people to afford. We missed Marissa this evening because she was feeling a bit under the weather. But the rest of us ordered various drinks from the menu. It felt nice to experience our company in a different, more relaxed setting, with our fancy cocktails. Just within four days of being away from my normal life, I realized how much I missed normalcy. I also realized how my normalcy was far away from the real, on-the-ground struggles of the majority of the population living under constrained economic situations. It was a guilty pleasure and privilege to forget about the reality and unfairness of the world and get lost in superficial yet fun topics such as Instagram pictures, joking about the drinks, recollecting several parties mishaps, and getting to know the lighter side of us.

Around 8.30 PM, the taxis that were arranged for us arrived and picked us up. Staying that late out in Chimbote, especially as foreigners, can be dangerous and I can imagine how much planning went into organizing this night for us to ensure we were safe yet be able to have fun. I was so grateful for this night.

I vividly remember the nonstop chatter and belly-aching laughs on our way back to the Parish and suddenly realized how sisterhood started bringing these strangers together.

ANCIENT RUINS TO INSTA STORIES

Day 5 – March 10, Tuesday, 2020

> *Breathe. Let go. And remind yourself that this very moment is the only one you have for sure.*
>
> *Oprah Winfrey*

CHAPTER 19

Being a tourist in a new place can mean both familiarity and uncertainty. A sense of excitement of not knowing what lies ahead in the day constantly exists. Inherently though that feeling is so familiar, because of all the times we have been tourists across the world.

That day, I think was rightly placed in the middle of the trip, to allow us to experience something familiar, exciting, and relaxing, to put on the tourist hat for a day.

We boarded the van at 7 AM with our breakfasts packed in our day bags. It was going to be a two-hour ride along with the good and the okay roads through diverse terrains to Trujillo, a beach town that was touristy and nearby. This was also to give us a flavor of the Peruvian beaches, food, and summer activities. Thanks to the first day of no one being sick; all of us from the group made it to the plan. I might have said this already, but I will say it again, there was not even a single dull moment when ML was around. The back half of the van was fully entertained with her stories followed by the conversations between the most entertaining duo Tanya and Adrian. Our second translator Adrian, a young, talented musician, and upcoming professional, who was a great addition to our group, joined us on this day trip to Trujillo. He ensured to make us laugh with his mostly real but sometimes made-up stories.

In what felt like no time, we reached our first destination – Huaca Del Sol, meaning the temple of the moon, built by the Moche civilization (100 CE to 800 CE). Investigations and archeological research were going on in this temple. Because of the dry climatic conditions, occasional heavy rainfalls, El Nino combined with looting from the Spanish invasion, the condition of the buildings were rustic and dusty, despite the restoration work. I have seen a number of ruins including Macchu Picchu, ruins along the Inca trail, and the Mayan ruins in Mexico. In comparison, this was less popular yet more natural and so it was not crowded.

It had been quite a few years since I experienced what I call scorching heat. After moving to Minnesota, my relationship with sun had become like the one with a childhood friend – we meet occasionally but always look forward to meeting again. But Peru put me back on my previous relationship with the sun, the one I was maintaining for most of my life growing up in tropical weather in India – like that really annoying supervisor, breathing fire down the neck, so I always hid away from any direct interactions.

We hired a tour guide who showed us around the ruins. While I really enjoyed the ancient stories, the archeological evidence, and mythological threads that held and continue to hold the cultural richness, an interesting piece of information that caught my attention is the name of a god from this temple. He is known as Iyeppayei (I do not know if this spelling is correct as I heard it verbally from our tour guide), the god of the mountains by the Moche people.

I do not have any details beyond the name to connect or understand whether, there is a relation to the Indian god, Iyeppa, who also sits in a mountain in Kerala, a southern state in India. If you, the reader, know more, write to me as I would be curious to know. This was just another factor that made me feel closer to the local culture.

Another funny incident took place while we were there. As we were finishing up the final section of the tour, there was a large wall that was full of patterns and designs which were being restored. Except for our group and the tour guide, there was no one in the area when we started the tour. But as we got closer to the wall, there was a man dressed up in clothes that looked out of place, maybe even out of time. We originally thought he was maybe carrying out a ritual in the temple. But as we got closer, we saw that he was not doing anything. It was both strange and funny, but we went about our way, listening to the history and taking pictures. Suddenly, this man walked toward us holding a giant cup, a huge crown, and a long lantern that looked ancient again. Not knowing how to react, not only because of the sudden encounter but also because of not knowing Spanish, some of us just stood there watching. All of us have our moments of weakness in life. For Karin and me, one of our weaknesses was that we could not control our laughter in a situation that we found funny. We looked at each other's faces, which did not help. So, we decided not to.

Meanwhile, the dressed-up middle-aged man talked to us in English. We were pleasantly surprised to know that he was offering to take a picture with us if we wanted and the antiques he was holding. We still don't know if he does that every day to add to the experience of visitors or we were just lucky to bump into him on that day. We made Anita, the queen of Chimbote, take a picture with this man and eventually got a group picture, too. And with that, our tour of the ruins ended as we said bye to our friend from the past era.

CHAPTER 20

Our next stop was Trujillo. But on the way, we stopped for a quick photoshoot realizing that this was the first day of the trip on which all of us made it to the plan. By the time we were done with group pics, solo pics, buddy pics, etc. we were all ready for lunch. The key highlight of the lunch was ceviche, a dish made from raw fish famous in Peru. Trujillo is in coastal Peru, which made ceviche even more special. Food, for many like me, is beyond just nutrition. Like a hug from a best friend or rain on a hot summer day; food is home. Food is comfort, one of the many comforts I thought I left behind when I left for Peru. This was because of the knowledge that we were not going to be eating in a restaurant that might offer multiple options. But as I said earlier, the kitchen crew proved me wrong and brought me the comfort of home food with whatever resources they had in place. But this day, we were in an area that was known for seafood and the primary agenda of this lunch was to taste the best ceviche in town. Joy found a restaurant that not only had ceviche but also tasty vegetarian options.

After a hearty meal, we went shopping for souvenirs. We took a stroll by the beach, some of our group members took a dip in the beach, while the rest of us walked, talked, and took lots of selfies. It was a good way to tire ourselves out physically and charge ourselves up mentally. Several months later, in 2021, I think about that day and I am sure none of us had any idea, that being on the beach with humans around us would never feel the same.

After taking a lot more sun than we needed, we nested back to the restaurant that offered us a table by the patio with a beach view and some of us settled with a cold drink. Tanya brought a fun card game with her called The Game. The warmth of the sun, the great company of women, engaging game, and a drink, sounds like a perfect getaway? It was.

Sometimes, I would be on the most awaited vacation, but my mind would not be fully present there. You know you are happy to be there, but a part of you counteracts the excitement for reasons unknown. I was experiencing this predominantly because part of me was elsewhere. At the back of my mind, there would be things running that were not in the present. The effect of experiencing a vacation like this is felt only after you get back home. You expect yourself to be energized by the trip, but the trip, the memories, and the visual images seem distant. It is there but the recollection of it does not bring back the excitement. I have experienced this too. What I am glad about though is that this day was not one of those days.

I am thankful that I was present there fully. My entire self was available there on that beach, with those friends, and my visual memory so intact and alive that in the following months of lockdown and COVID-19, I recollected this image so many times and felt the warmth on my skin and tasted the sangria on my mouth that smiled.

CHAPTER 21

One would think that the ride back was probably quiet from everyone taking a nap after a long tiring day. But no, not in this group. As we were heading back, ML, being new to Instagram, started asking questions about Instagram stories. I was new to Instagram and in fact, I started using it a lot more. inspired by the group. Tanya, being the more experienced in using Instagram, started helping ML, which ended up becoming hour-long coaching on Instagram tips. The contrast of that day starting from ancient stories to ending the day with Instagram stories was nothing less than fun.

We reached the Parish, reminiscing on all that we did today, looking forward to a simple meal, and gearing ourselves up for a packed day the next morning. We all had a distant understanding of what was starting to happen in other countries due to COVID-19 and were discussing briefly as a happy hour chat on our usual patio on what kind of complications this might bring. Just when you think life is starting to get complicated, life tells you that "You have no idea what complication can look like" and shows you what it is. That was what was waiting for us the next day as we woke up to a world that was about to change forever.

GIVING BACK AND SHARING STORIES

Day 6 – March 11, Wednesday, 2020

> *Success isn't about how much money you make. It's about the difference you make in people's lives.*
>
> Michelle Obama

CHAPTER 22

I woke up to an email from my company that a work from home order has been put in place for the entire company, starting next week. My company, 150 years old, has grown on a culture of in-person connections, relationships and the entire company working from home meant, that COVID-19 had escalated beyond what we could perceive in that remote town of Peru. We also woke up to the news of border closures between Europe, the US, and potentially other countries along the way. Some in the group had planned for extended stays in Peru for vacation and this news worried them. There was a general concern developing amongst us, though none of us spent enough time thinking or talking about it. Our packed agenda made sure of that.

There were two plans for the day – one was to paint a section of the Parrish we stayed in and the other was to visit the jewelry workshop for the last time to spend time with the artisan partners.

For the first half of the day, we were taken into an event hall, which had to be dusted and painted. What

I liked about all the volunteering activities we did was that they were just enough challenging that there was real progress made and also gave us the satisfaction of contributing to a real need. The activity itself started on a high note, with loud music, Jessica and Karin's fun dance moves, and a coordinated team effort to get that done as soon as possible. It was a big hall with a lot of surface area to be painted. Everyone started getting their hands dirty and, in the excitement, I forgot to cover my nose. I am allergic to dust, and the escalation of its effect happened quickly. So, I could not continue beyond a certain time as the room started to get actively dusty. We also had some external volunteers to help us with the work as the area was huge, including some work needed in the ceiling. With enough hands on the work, I came back to the room. I was later filled in with all the fun and chaos that happened in that event hall so that I wouldn't miss out on anything.

CHAPTER 23

Because this is the final visit to the workshop, Karin was going to take pictures of all artisan partners with their families. It was her beautiful idea to get this arranged through Joy, so these women and their families have a memorable family picture hanging in their homes. This thoughtful human never fails to put a smile on my face. So, we all dressed up, relatively better than previous days, and got to the workshop.

There were three different activities planned for our final visit to make this day memorable for us and the artisan partners. First, the artisan women were given the challenge to design their own jewelry and display it for us. This was exclusively for us to shop directly from them, looking through their individual designs. It was of course for a group of jewelry enthusiasts, so what was there to not love about that? What was even more moving was to see Joy. The pride and happiness on her face to see this group of artisan partners design their own jewelry to the quality standards that they have today showed that this was nothing less than a journey of hard work and perseverance.

After we were done with the shopping, each of us from the group was to write a positive adjective word that describes one person from the artisan woman group and vice versa. There was translation required on both ends to coordinate this activity for which, our translators Adrian, Claudia, and our very own Joy did an amazing job.

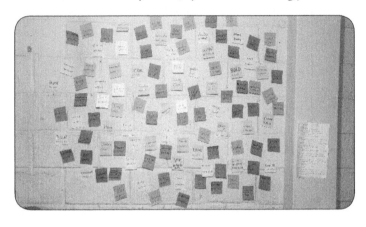

Rubi, an artisan woman, gave me the word 'Reliable'. Whether she saw some aspect of reliability in me, I do not know. But it felt good to hold that word in my hand, to include it in my 'to-be' list. What resonated the most with me was that when all of us wrote down the words and put them up on the wall, the humble wall that stayed invisible till then, suddenly became the wall of power, that could not be missed; just like the growth of women working day and night inside those walls.

CHAPTER 24

The best is always saved for the last. We were geared up for our final activity in the workshop.

Our final and most awaited activity was for us to interview the artisan partners. Two from our group were paired with one artisan partner and there was a translator assigned to each group. ML and I were paired with Elena and Rosario, two completely different women yet connected through a common thread of love for jewelry and their family. Adrian was assigned as our translator and as a group, we started the interviews with our assigned women artisans.

Elena is a survivor! An exceptionally hardworking and inspiring woman from Chimbote, Elena raised her two daughters (one of them specially-abled) by herself. To earn enough money to get by, Elena cleaned houses, made (and still does) these incredibly tasty chips from scratch to sell in the market and at an event, and washed laundry for income. With Fair Anita, her life has taken a turn for the better allowing more time with Jessica, her daughter, and more money for her care. Elena has been working with this group for 2 years, earrings being her favorite, but hopes for more design in the future. She lives and breathes the advice she received from her leader Maritza, who was the primary inspiration behind Elena's jewelry-making career. Her next goal is to travel to Lima someday soon to visit her other daughter and two grandchildren.

Rosario is a loving mother of four and bracelet expert in the Fair Anita artisan network from Peru. She has a specially-abled son, Caesar (26), who was healthy when born, but due to improper diagnosis by local healthcare professionals for an infection, his condition worsened. Rosario is thankful to god for the miracle of saving her son. However, due to the delayed treatment, some of his everyday abilities were impacted. The family's financial positioning worsened due to ongoing treatment. She is grateful to Fair Anita for her ability to earn more money for his care meanwhile having the ability to take time out for her aging husband and son.

After some laughter, tears, hugs, and pictures, our interviews came to end. Their stories were powerful, moving and showcased how far these women would go for their families. Also, Elena and Rosario were just two of the other brave and strong women in the room. Rubi! Maria! Marie Carmen! So many more! Other group interviews were still going on, so our group silently settled down in the workshop. As I was looking through my notes and digesting everything that was shared, Joy asked if someone could volunteer to interview one last artisan left – Maritza. Till date, I thank the universe for this moment and how lucky I was to get that opportunity. ML and I, done with our scheduled interviews, jumped at this opportunity. Joy, herself became our translator, as other translators were still occupied. Karin joined us to take a video of Maritza's interview. This was also the last day we will get to spend time with Maritza on that trip as she was going to Lima the next day for a surgery she needed to undergo.

Maritza is a leader and one of the faces of Fair Anita. She fought against all odds to achieve what has now become this growing women's workshop in Chimbote, Peru, which she calls "the little workshop with the big heart". The artisans meet in her home, where she can continue to encourage & manage, teach jewelry-making skills, and nurture leadership in others. One of her guiding principles has been to prove that this can be done, that disability (Maritza is a wheelchair user, and has consistent dialysis treatments) is not an excuse and we shouldn't allow prejudice to keep us down. As she says, "I gotta do it, because if I don't do it, I'm not Maritza", and she continues to instill that determination in all the women working with her! Maritza's growing workshop is not only supporting her livelihood but allowing her to share this commitment and drive with other women in the community. With Fair Anita, her vision is to create and lead a cooperative of fifty women and share her joy of making jewelry with more women. In short, she felt to me like a superwoman grandma (mine were and are too!)

There is no way I can do justice to her words through my expression here. As I sat there and listened to her speak, tears poured down my eyes and I was transfixed on her charisma, her smile, despite her trembling voice. Each word came like a bullet out of a gun, sharp and focused. My mind kept asking what this woman was doing there in that tiny part of Peru. She was not trained in leadership skills, public speaking, management principles, but at that moment I understood that she never needed any of those to be the leader she had always been. A part of me wanted the trip to end on this highest note. I am sure there are several inspiring women like Maritza in our lives and around us, so as a reader, this might not create the same effect that this experience had on me. But the impacts of seeing her being there in her environment, getting a glimpse of everyday lives, and yet, the energy she brings to people around her, cannot be described in words.

I am glad I met Maritza and she will always be in a corner of my heart, waiting to give me a nudge, if I ever need a dose of motivation in my life. The rest of that night, I don't think I remember very well, maybe because I consciously wanted to carry that high to sleep.

MARKET TO TABLE

Day 7 – March 12, Thursday, 2020

*The question isn't who is going to let me.
It is who is going to stop me.*

Ayn Rand

CHAPTER 25

Waking up to the official last day of the trip was bittersweet. Bitter because of how quickly the days went by and how much I will miss the company of these incredible women. Sweet only because of the content feeling from everything and everyone I gained in the trip. The anxiety around COVID-19 was still not felt in Chimbote except in our phones. The only theme of the day was food. This was a day to say thanks and goodbyes to the community that welcomed and took care of us with wide smiles and warm hearts. And we were going to do that by going to the local food market, shopping for the ingredients ourselves, and coming back to cook together.

We took a stroll around Chimbote for one last time led by our ever-energetic Anita. The market was very similar to what I had experienced in India. Several open shops next to each other, occupying a wide range of options for vegetables, meat, other groceries, flowers, etc. The friendly chatters of vendors, the scent that was so unique to such open markets took me back to my days in

. This scenery inspired Karin to do a photoshoot for r Anita jewelry. Most importantly, we were the models. What a fun experience! When someone asks me why I like Fair Anita, I always struggle to provide a brief answer. It is probably because of several such tiny experiences that make me connect and feel personal with their brand. I did not have to look, smile, or stand a certain way to be their model. So, I did model for a newly launched *Interconnection Horn and Wood Necklace* with a wide grin and a little more boosted confidence.

There was a lot of "Look at the apples!", "Feel the potatoes!", "Touch the earring!", "Smell the lemons!", all in the name of posing. Obviously, our photographer was behind all of it. The market vendors I am sure had a lot of fun watching us clowns walk around the market with a camera like we were in Disneyland. Finally, it was time to head back and start cooking. If you feel like spending more time in this market, head straight to the Fair Anita website and check out their pictures. An added challenge for you is, if you end up finding all the pictures taken in this market, and genuinely end up not buying anything for yourself, I say you have the best willpower to resist any temptations in the world.

With the help of Anita, her crew, and our superwomen group, cooking was completed quickly, and everyone got ready for the very final event of this trip with the Chimbote artisan women.

CHAPTER 26

All of us were really excited about the final party, to spend quality time, and to say goodbye to the men and women who made our stay happen. The party was organized in the basketball court right next to the Parish. Tables and chairs were arranged, speakers and music were ready, all the artisan women started arriving with their families, we were all dressed up and all set. The weather was perfect with a nice breeze. Even amidst the loud music, chit chats, honking of cars, there was calm and peace that I felt. Everything went as per the plan so far. In fact, I had no idea how quickly the time went by. Slowly, everyone settled on their seats and the dance performances began. There were three dance performances that were authentic to the Peruvian culture. I do not know the names of those dance forms, unfortunately. Women dressed in full white wavy dress, with puffed full sleeves, hair made into two-sided braids with a white hat, and a piece of multicolor scarf-like garment worn diagonally across the chest. They had been rehearsing for this performance late in the nights after finishing up their day jobs. Yes, we met some of the sweetest humans on earth. The dance performance that started gracefully, moved quickly into a dance party which included all of us dancing our hearts out.

We then served the dinner our group cooked for the guests. Shortly, it was time to end the party. Lots of Peruvian-style goodbyes which meant lots of hugging and kissing while the rest of the world was freaking out with social distancing. Some of them, with tears in their eyes, said long goodbyes and I did not have any translator next to me, so I didn't know still don't know what they told me. But love was communicated, happiness was exchanged, and goodbyes were completed. It was the best farewell to the beautiful bonds formed.

SYMPATHY TO EMPATHY

Day 7 – March 12, Thursday, 2020

> *I don't want to ever sell something based off of pity. Pity creates an intense power dynamic between the artisan and the consumer. We want to build empathetic relationships instead.*
>
> Joy McBrien, Founder of Fair Anita

CHAPTER 27

Why I think Joy organized this trip...

Only toward the end of the trip, I understood. I remember the sympathy and pity I felt the first time we were in a room with the artisan women, listening to their stories. And that final day, as I waved goodbyes, I had a deep sense of understanding, empathy, and inspiration toward the women. Empathy is to put yourself in someone else's shoes. According to me, empathy is the ability to understand other's feelings without necessarily putting their life in a position that is better or worse in comparison to yours. It is hard to explain the feeling when you know their life is harder than yours, yet you do not feel pity, rather an overwhelming sense of respect comes for them and the work they do. I practically experienced, what the difference was to give out of pity and to give out of respect.

I realized that there will always be someone who has more money than we do and someone who has less. If I do not want to be treated with pity by someone who has more than what I have, then I have no right to do the same to others.

I am glad I experienced this change in mindset because it would have been harder to grapple with the emotions if I was left just with pity for them. What is wrong with pity? Nothing. In fact, I think it is absolutely natural to feel pity for someone who does not have what we have. But it is important to watch out for the slippery slope that gets us into creating power dynamics. All of us work because we need money to survive. Whether our primary motivation to work is money or passion or both, do you think it should matter to the consumer of your work? I want to be recognized for the results, not for my motivation. And I want to be fairly compensated, for the work I do. When I am buying something from someone out of pity, I am unconsciously assuming that the seller's primary motivation is money and that's what I think creates the power dynamics.

Next time, you buy something from someone out of pity, think about this. If you felt anything different based on what you read here, please write to me. I would be forever grateful that you chose to share a moment of reflection from your life with me.

This might seem so small, yet it can make a world of difference once you experience the difference. When I turned my focus from sympathy to empathy, I noticed that I stopped thinking about how unfair the world is. I stopped trying to find a solution to fix the problems. Because in reality, there is no single solution that can fix any of the world's problems. With empathy, I experienced peace within myself. I started seeing their life for what they are, in all their unfairness. And I started noticing myself taking tiny steps toward the direction of what a fair world should look like.

Just for this experience, I owe a special thanks to Joy.

CHAPTER 28

Why I think I signed up for this trip...

For the outside world, I was part of a big extended family. But within me, it had always been a small world made of my parents and my brother, later my husband. I didn't need to go out because I thought what I had was perfect. But my only sibling died. In the days followed by his death, I used to desperately look for him everywhere. I used to look for him in my friends, his friends, people I met. I missed him. But more than that, I realized how big of a space he occupied in my life. I felt that my world shrank so small even though it was less by only one. And in those days, I used to wonder so much about whether it was possible for anyone to create that kind of family-like bond outside their homes. I had not seen or known the world enough to believe that such bonds existed. I have a LOT of great humans in my life who were and are brothers, sisters, and family to me. But I kept telling myself during those times that by looking for a family-like feeling, outside the family I was born with, I am only cheating myself to compensate for my loss. But the day we arrived in Chimbote I saw that it was possible through Joy. She calls Chimbote her second home, Anita, her mom, and a lot of women there as her sisters. And I saw that those were not just words. She was at her second home. And that made me believe that my world is bigger than what I thought it was. Her story inspired confidence in me that the bonds I created outside my tiny world, are in fact real.

Since that Day 1, I had come a long way on that trip. As we gathered together after the party for our final reflection activity, I realized how close the women in my group have become to me. How much we got to know each other. How much we had adjusted for each other to make this trip experience as smooth as possible. And I realized suddenly why I came on this trip.

Fair Trade was new to me, so I did not sign up because I was passionate about Fair Trade. Cultural experience, maybe yes, but it was not the selling factor for me especially because of where I come from and how similar I have seen Peru to be. To help someone – definitely, no! I knew that I am probably burdening the locals more than helping, by being there and having them do all that extra work for me. Then, what was it? Well, other than the fact that I wanted to travel alone, it was the connections I made there! The women I met and made friends on the trip shared a commonality with me now. We were the only group of women to have experienced this trip that exact way and that can never be taken away. It was done. The bonds were made. The women from Peru, I will remember and continue to get inspired by and support them from afar but is it highly likely that I would not see them again. But this group of women is different. Some of them stay few miles away from me and some of them may be a few hundred miles away. Other than sharing space for ten days, we shared a bond so close, filled with moments of vulnerability, laughter, tears, and many more that could not be undone. I knew that I will be in touch with these women and I do till date. At that moment, I knew that I would go back home to my world that just got a tiny bit bigger.

As we went back to our rooms for the last night of our stay there, I was overwhelmed with all that I thought of and never communicated. Going through grief has taught one key lesson. Memories can fade away very soon as life goes by so fast. So, it is very important to document our memories. I consider myself to be more expressive when I write. So, I decided to write a note to each of my fellow women, so they know how much I appreciated every one of their presence. Deep discussions about life & relationship with Tanya, the concept of home, reflections with Jessica, about our personality traits, interpersonal family relationships, and lessons from ML, art as a medium for change from Karin, so many Fair Trade one-on-ones with Marissa, Sue, Grayce, dealing with the trip experiences with Julia, about the cutest golden doodles with Sarah, about everything under the sun with Joy – these could not be possibly expressed in conversations. At least, I could not. So, I wrote everything out.

The next morning, our final plan in the itinerary was to hike up a small mountain next to our Parish and then head back to Lima to catch our flights. I stayed up late and wrote those notes, so I could hand them over to them over the mountain when we all soak up Chimbote for one last time. And then, I went to sleep wishing for the morning to come sooner, so I could give these notes to everyone. I shouldn't have wished for it!

FINALE PLAN

Day 8 – March 13, Friday, 2020

How Our Trip Ended – Expectation

All of us went up the mountains to enjoy the sunrise scenery. I shared my little notes with all of them. Everyone hugged each other and took lots of pictures. Finally, we all got ready and boarded the bus. A week later, safely, everyone got back home.

How Our Trip Ended – Reality

At 7.30 AM we were all supposed to board the van that would take us to the hiking point. It was around 7 AM I think, I was in the shower. I got out in frenzy hoping I did not take too long and someone else was not waiting outside for me. The room was quiet, partially empty. I still thought most of them would have gown down already and that I was late. I am always paranoid about being late because I lose a sense of time in the shower. But Sue broke the news to me. She said our leader Joy was robbed outside the Parish.

In a state of confusion, I rushed downstairs. That's when I saw that she was not just robbed, but also dragged down by someone in the taxi until her bag broke off and she was left there down the road with scratches and thankfully some minor injuries. I could not process that yet. I still cannot. Especially, because she was seen as one among the locals. She calls Chimbote her second home. So, I couldn't make sense of anything. I rushed down and she was over the phone sorting out several things like her phone, cards, bank, letting her parents know, and her passport. For some time, I tried to help where I could, we all did. We were all angry sad and *shocked* that this happened. And what was even more shocking was that this was a planned attack.

As she was gathering herself back and trying to think next steps, she was brave enough to still care for us and asked us to get ready. With her passport lost, her cards and phone gone, she registered a police complaint and joined us with a spare phone to head to the bus.

Just while I was packing my bag, I saw the notes that I was supposed to give to everyone. After deep contemplation, I silently slid the notes under everyone's bags, without creating a lot of attention to it. I still do not know if what I did was mindful of that situation or not. But I assumed that even if not right away, they might appreciate the documentation of our memories sometime later once we were all out of the shock. We got our bags packed and got ready to leave, still processing that unfortunate situation, still not believing how everything turned upside down in a few minutes.

I would not get into all the details of the robbery or what came after because that is not my story. What I can share though is my experience of that incident. Few things kept crossing my mind the entire day.

1. If this incident happened a day before, all ten of our passports would have gone with Joy's.

2. The reality of what it means for a woman to get out of her world and make change happen.

3. The impact of this incident on her.

Growing up as a girl was not simple for me. My body is always in fight or flight mode when I am outside. It takes a long time to recover from that. My body still gets stressed out when I am outside in India in a public place. Lesser than before maybe because now I go in groups always and I go out mostly for fun when I go on a vacation now. But growing up, trains were an overnight means of transport to get us from one place to another. And I have never slept well once because of my fear of someone doing something bad to me while I am sleeping. Going out shopping in busy streets meant a high possibility of being groped. Walking in the dark in a less crowded place meant being afraid of something worse. It is not possible to completely get out of these traumatic experiences. In my mind, I might have done a better job of getting out, but my body still carries the trauma and reacts involuntarily to such situations where it senses the risk. Standing in broad daylight outside the church might never mean the same to Joy after that incident and that hurts me the most.

Having lost her passport and amidst COVID-19 lockdown, Joy was stuck there for a month. ML, who extended her trip for a few days for the Amazon experience, also couldn't make it back on time and ended up being stuck in a hotel in Lima for 2-3 weeks. Jessica and Grayce barely made it on time and somehow got into the US before all hell broke loose with COVID-19. All of us who got back were thankful that we made it back home. We hardly had any time to process the trip, as we came back to a different world that demanded a lot more from us. For several weeks, I could not bring myself to translate that experience into words. Eventually, as I gradually started looking at my journals and started reflecting on how I felt before and after the trip, I knew that I had already changed. And maybe that's why it was that hard to make sense of the change.

Violence against women was and is an area that affects me deeply. In fact, that was the cause, that made me go on this trip. Before this experience, I had a lot of questions about why the world is the way it is. I used to spend a lot of time thinking more about the cause and the solutions. I was fueled by anger, frustration, and a multitude of emotions when I come across news about any violent actions against women. While the emotions are still the same, after the trip, I started understanding the complexity of the issue. I realized how deeply patriarchy is influencing the lives of every man and woman, including myself, my family, friends, and people around me. I could also see how much we are all fighting against it, directly and indirectly.

Some of us who are privileged enough to realize at least that patriarchy exists, realize that we have choices in life, and are fighting for those choices. Even after realizing our choices, some of us might be living in situations where we cannot execute those choices. But what if a major or minor (I do not know) part of the world does not even know that there are different choices in life? Not because of ignorance but because in their bubble of society, there truly is no choice for them!

As social animals, we all fight to belong somewhere. I look at several life-altering events such as marriage or parenting as a choice. Someone like me can still belong in my social bubble because I personally know men and women who think like me. But if the bubble I lived in was so small, that I am the only person to look for a choice, how far can I go with my choices? How long can I survive before I am broken by the pressure to belong? Rather, if the bubble is where I have grown up all my life, hell, do I even know that I have other choices? These deep-rooted impressions on who men and women are supposed to be, trickles, rather pours down into every single aspect of our lives today beyond what we consciously realize.

I understood that gender equality is a complex issue. And my key takeaway from this experience was that grassroots-level changes and efforts in every aspect of life are equally important. Celebrating Women's day is as important as the representation of women in politics. Push for women leaders in corporate is as important as the fight for equal education for girls. Raising responsible men is as important as raising women. Fighting against gender-based violence is as important as fighting for policies and laws toward monitoring cybercrime. Any action is better than no action. No action is too small. This is true for any social injustice that deeply bothers us and leaves us feeling helpless. How will this small action from me fix this problem, you ask? Yes, one action alone does not lead to the solution, but one drop does not make an ocean either.

This trip was not one with a bed full of roses. It had its fair share of challenges, discomforts, pushing me out of my comfort zone yet equally rewarding me with deep cultural and humane, learning experiences. That is precisely why this trip had the power to stop me from searching for the ocean and convinced me to become a drop instead.

Hey YOU!

Thank you for being the tiny drops,

You might not be able to see the ocean today

But it is only because you are a part of it.

Stop looking for the sun to get you up to the clouds,

One sun is not enough for us.

Let's build our own wings,

And help each other build wings.

So, one day, when it is time to fly,

We can rise above the ocean,

Look below,

And be thankful that,

The tiny invisible drops did what they could!

EPILOGUE

She, the tiny drop, did what she knew the best. She believed in her voice and went on to write "Beads that Lead".

ACKNOWLEDGMENTS

I feel incredibly lucky to have experienced this life-changing trip, right before the world changed forever with COVID-19. This experience helped in shaping my perceptions and thoughts during the lockdown and everything that followed.

Thanks to the incredible group of women Tanya, Jessica, Julia, Marissa, Sue, Sarah, Grayce, Mary Lind, Karin who accompanied me, without whom these experiences would not have existed. Thanks to Fair Anita, Joy, Anita, Lica, Maritza, and the entire Chimbote crew who worked and prepared so hard to make this experience a safe, memorable one for us.

After I came back from the trip, I shared a portion of this journey on Facebook. I am forever thankful to my dear friend, mentor, motivator, marketing guru and an author himself, Pravin Shekar for encouraging and pushing me to write this experience as a book. I doubted myself and still do, but I continued with it nevertheless to keep up my promise for him. And standing on the other side of my experience of writing this book, I am really glad I did. The writing process of this book greatly helped me reflect on my experiences and process the varied array of emotions. Thanks to my friend and author Pavithra Krishna Prasad for the pep talk during a time I was about to give up on this book. It really helped me persist and complete the first draft. Thanks to Suji, Meenu, Anu, Viji, Suja for this group significantly influenced me and constantly encouraged me to pursue writing as an art form to express my thoughts. Thanks to Indrajith, Prabhu, Kausi, Vikram, Yuva, Karups, Vivek Anand, Sugi, and many such wonderful friends I missed to identify here who always took out time to read, provide feedback and encourage me. Thanks to many friends, brothers, sisters, who continue to play a significant role in increasing my trust in myself.

'Thank you' is not enough to appreciate my partner in everything, Prashanth, who introduced me to Fair Anita, and continually encourages me to push my limitations; my first critic and the best motivator. He was beyond supportive during all those hours of writing, brainstorming, and rewriting. Grateful for all the yummy food he cooked for me to keep me energized and focused while I was writing. Last but not least special thanks to my beautiful parents, Sekar and Usha, for everything you have done and continue to do for me. I am thankful to inherit your values and wisdom that continue to guide me in challenging times. After going through a terrible tragedy in your lives, you have risen above the struggles and inspire so many young and old ones around you. I am grateful to my mom who aspires to evolve and adapt to this ever-changing world and to my dad who embodies hard work and sincerity in anything he does. The independent woman I am today, with the clarity of mind to stand up for what's right in the world is only because of the seeds that were sown through their genes and upbringing.

A treat-filled thanks to our pup Jager, who was so obedient while I was away on this trip and always stayed by my side while writing this book.

My forever thanks to my brother who was the first-ever human to challenge me in life and will remain to be the most special one who taught me several valuable lessons. And I am forever grateful for and proud of everything he accomplished in his twenty-four years of presence, as well as the wisdom he left behind for me through his absence. He proved that age is nothing but a number through his maturity and actions. He touched way too many lives in the short period of time he lived, and I aspire every day to become the mature, courageous, selfless friend that he was.

We miss you, sister!

Special mention to Maria, one of the artisan women. As we publish this book, she has lost her battle against COVID-19. She was full of life and laughter filled with kindness and love. My prayers for her family to cope with the loss of this beautiful soul. She was a proud and inspirational mother and other than that, below are some of the many good things she will be remembered for by all of us who formed a special bond with her during our stay.

ABOUT THE AUTHOR

Harini, born in India, currently residing in the US, is a supply chain professional by the day and writer by the night. Her love for writing began when she started writing letters and poems to her close ones to express herself more deeply. This helped her discover the joy of writing, which after several years of self-doubt, has finally manifested in the form of her first book "Beads that Lead". She calls herself a small fish in the ocean of writing, just learning to swim. Encourage her, help her learn, and cheer for her so she can keep you entertained for a lot more years to come!

Made in the USA
Monee, IL
24 March 2021